A Skateboarding Story

PRAISE FOR *STORYSHARES*

"One of the brightest innovators and game-changers in the education industry."
– Forbes

"Your success in applying research-validated practices to promote literacy serves as a valuable model for other organizations seeking to create evidence-based literacy programs."

- Library of Congress

"We need powerful social and educational innovation, and Storyshares is breaking new ground. The organization addresses critical problems facing our students and teachers. I am excited about the strategies it brings to the collective work of making sure every student has an equal chance in life."
– Teach For America

"Around the world, this is one of the up-and-coming trailblazers changing the landscape of literacy and education."
- International Literacy Association

"It's the perfect idea. There's really nothing like this. I mean wow, this will be a wonderful experience for young people."   - Andrea Davis Pinkney, Executive Director, Scholastic

"Reading for meaning opens opportunities for a lifetime of learning. Providing emerging readers with engaging texts that are designed to offer both challenges and support for each individual will improve their lives for years to come. Storyshares is a wonderful start."
- David Rose, Co-founder of CAST & UDL

A Skateboarding Story

Tammy Griffith

STORYSHARES

Story Share, Inc.
New York. Boston. Philadelphia

Storyshares
Story Share, Inc.
24 N. Bryn Mawr Avenue #340
Bryn Mawr, PA 19010-3304
www.storyshares.org

Inspiring reading with a new kind of book.

Interest Level: Middle School
Grade Level Equivalent: 3.3

9781642611274

Book design by Storyshares

Printed in the United States of America

Storyshares Presents

1

My friends and I spent a lot of time on the streets, skateboarding and hanging out. It seemed like we were always in trouble or running from it, the three of us. No one really wanted kids around, especially kids on skateboards.

We spent a lot of time competing with each other or learning new tricks. Sometimes we dared each other to do stupid stuff because we were bored. Someone would make a dare, and the other two would jump in to see who was the bravest. A dare led me to Miss Wanda Rose.

Terence was the oldest, on his second year of

tenth grade. He was tall and skinny, with smooth brown skin and sad eyes. He always wore a black beret and headphones. That was his style. He liked to talk loud and be the center of attention. His way of intimidating people was to stand really close to them so they had to look up at him. It worked for the other kids, but for Lark and me, we just laughed and pushed him back. We were a street family.

Lark was a true tomboy. She liked anything that was a challenge or got her dirty. She was almost as good on a skateboard as me, but she learned the tricks before I could.

She wasn't afraid to fall off her board or get a scrape, but after she learned a trick, she usually got bored and moved on to something else. She was taller than me and never without her pink snapback hat turned to the back. Sometimes she wore her hair in a ponytail, but most of the time it just spilled out from under her cap, wild curls flying everywhere. Lark liked pink, but she would put her fist in your face if you called her a girly girl.

And then there was me. I was the shortest of the three of us. I didn't really have a style like Terence and Lark.

My mom didn't make much money and my dad

wouldn't help us, so jeans and a t-shirt were about all I had. I was always wearing holes in the sides and toes of my shoes from doing skateboard tricks.

The three of us were always a team, always together. After school, we stayed out till dark and sometimes later. Our parents worked and never seemed to have any time for us, so we learned how to be a family together. Terence's mom worked two jobs, one cleaning buildings and one at a grocery store. Lark's dad sold some kind of machine parts, and my mom was a hair stylist.

We didn't need adults. We had each other. Well, at least that's what we thought. Adults seemed to nag us about anything we did. Our clothes weren't right, our hair wasn't right, the skateboarding was too annoying or too loud. Why did we spend so much time together? Didn't we have anything else to do? There were always endless questions and harsh looks from adults.

I loved to skateboard. It was a challenge to learn new tricks. An Ollie, a Kick Flip, a Pop Shuvit, a Nose Manual. We didn't have a skateboard park near us, so we used whatever we could find to do tricks on.

A curb, a staircase, a railing: they were spots to

learn new tricks. But if some adult came out of their house and yelled at us, we moved on to another place.

We skated through the neighborhood, playing a game called SKATE, where one person does a trick and the others have to copy it. If you miss the trick, you get an S, then a K, and so on. Lark showed off her Ollie, popping the board high in the air as she skated up onto the curb. I followed her, sticking it. Terence did the same.

Next, she did a Kick Flip. She pushed her back foot down on the back edge of the board with her front foot in the center of the board. Her front foot kicked backwards in an attempt to get the board to flip over long ways and land back in place. She missed it and the board landed upside down and she stumbled backwards, almost falling.

I tried the Kick Flip and almost stuck it, but my foot slipped off the back of the board when I landed. Terence, who was really better than we were at skateboarding, stuck the trick.

Terence gave us a break and did a Pop Shuvit.

He pushed his back foot, making the board pop up in the air and spin 180 degrees around, landing back on the board. Lark barely managed to stick it, falling off the board after the three second rule. If we could stay on the board for three seconds after a trick, it was considered good. I also made it, even though I came really close to the curb and had to turn quickly to avoid crashing into it.

It was my turn next and I did a Nose Manual. It was my favorite trick. My front foot was on the front edge of the board. As I skated by, I pushed my foot down and skated on the two front wheels.

We all counted out loud, one-two-three-four-five! I made it five seconds before I went down on all four wheels. It was a record for me.

"Yes!" I shouted, pumping my fists in the air.

"Dude, that was sick!" said Lark.

Terence was even impressed and gave me a high five.

We finished the game and skated around on the street. Then Lark dared me to Ollie higher than her. She did an Ollie, her skateboard going up about a foot in the air.

Then it was my turn. I got in position and popped my foot as hard as I could, not wanting to lose. My skateboard jumped high in the air, and I could see

Terence open his mouth wide with surprise as I flew by him. When I landed heavily in the middle of my board, I heard a sharp snap. I could feel the board cave in under my feet and I fell hard on my right arm. I was scraped from my elbow to my wrist. It really hurt, but I wouldn't let anyone know how bad it felt.

That night, I asked my mom for money for a new skateboard.

"You shouldn't have been so foolish with your skateboard, Luke," she fussed, as she wiped my arm with a wet cloth. There were pieces of dirt and pavement still in my arm and she scrubbed to get them out. "You're lucky you didn't break your neck!"

She ran her hands through my blonde hair, trying to make it part off to the side. But when she took her hand away, I shook my head and let it fall back in my eyes.

"We never had any money," I said. "I've had that skateboard for two years and you promised to get me new one at Christmas, but you didn't." I was angry and I couldn't help it. My next words probably should have stayed in my mouth, but they tumbled out before I could think. "You are never around and all I have is my friends. You are never here for me and you are so selfish to not even get me a new board. Now I'll have nothing to do all summer!"

My mother was not a screamer like some parents. When she was mad, she got really quiet. She straightened up from cleaning my arm and walked out of the room. I knew I'd hurt her. I knew that things were really hard because my dad never gave us any money.

But all I could think of was how much I needed a new board.

2

Lark had an old skateboard she said I could borrow, but it was narrow and I couldn't seem to do anything on it but go forward.

The trucks were worn out and it hardly moved when I shifted my weight to turn. I gave up trying to skate on it. Terence and Lark decided to take a day off from skateboarding to walk around with me. Lark said it was because she was bored with skating, but I knew they felt bad for me.

"Hey, Luke, my mom gave me five bucks," Terence said. "Want to walk to the gas station and get a hot dog?"

"Walk all that way? It must be like five miles or something," I said. I was still angry over breaking my skateboard and embarrassed that my friends were walking because I had no wheels.

"Don't be a baby," said Lark. "I'm starving!"

We walked to the store and got three hot dogs and a 2-Liter bottle of soda. As we walked back towards our neighborhood, we stopped in front of an abandoned house. It was a white 2-story building with a sagging roof and a couple of busted-out windows.

We sat down on the steps that led up to the house. Lark and I sat sideways on the steps so we could share the soda and look at the old house. Terence stood on the sidewalk, bored.

"That's a creepy old house," said Lark, pretending to shiver and rubbing her arms.

"Bet you wouldn't go inside," I teased her. "Probably get eaten by a giant rat or a starving homeless guy." I held my arms up and made my hands into claws, bared my teeth and growled.

She threw her hot dog wrapper at me and pretended to be mad.

Terrance laughed at us and challenged me next. "Why don't you throw a rock and bust out a window?"

My stomach knotted. I liked a challenge, but this was someone's house, even if it was abandoned. But I couldn't go back on a dare. Of course, he hadn't actually said the word *dare* yet.

Lark chimed in, "That's a great idea. I *dare* you!"

Well, now it was for real. I didn't have much in my life. I wasn't rich, popular, or handsome. One of my eyes was a little lazy and sometimes people stared at me funny. I kept my hair long to hang over that eye in case anyone was looking too close. In school, I barely got passing grades. My mother and the teachers just never took much time to explain things that were hard for me to get, so I gave up and guessed a lot. But at least I had my honor. I couldn't turn down a dare.

Well, I also didn't have a juvenile record, which I could end up with if I got caught busting out windows.

"I'm not going to throw rocks at some stupid, old house," I said, taking a drink of the soda and wiping my mouth. I tried to look as cool as I could. "Besides, my mom said I had to be home early today to clean my room. She's really mad about my busted skateboard," I lied. I sat back against the stairs to see if it was going to work.

"I think you're a big chicken," laughed Terence. "A real mama's boy." He leaned over me and took the bottle from me as if to tell me he was now in control.

"Well, I have to hurry up because I gotta get home. But I'll throw one rock." I looked around in the grass for the smallest stone I could find.

Before I could find anything, Lark spoke up. "Here's a nice one, mama's boy!" She handed me what looked like a boulder. I took it from her hand. I threw the rock at the house and it hit the wall to the left of a second story window.

"Way to go, Jeter," Terence said. "Try it again." This time the rock was even larger.

"Could you have found something a little bigger?" I rolled my eyes at him as I took the rock. This time I chucked the rock as hard as I could so I could get it over with and get out of there fast. I was ready to run as soon as I heard the broken glass. The rock felt so heavy in my hand and my heart was pounding.

3

It was a woman's scream that came next, as if she'd been hit by the rock. I stood there, stunned. How could that be?

Terence and Lark heard it, too, and they took off for home.

My legs were frozen in place as I listened to the last of the glass tinkling down onto the porch. A dog barked in the distance. I heard what sounded like a woman talking and moaning inside the house, but I wasn't sure.

And then my legs unglued from the sidewalk and I bolted down the street as fast as I could run. When I felt I was at a safe distance, I ducked beside a building and fell against the wall, breathing hard. *Did I hit someone? With the rock?*

Wasn't the house abandoned? What if she saw me? What if she knew me? I was in so much trouble.

I stopped thinking about myself for a moment and thought about the woman. *Did I really hear a woman scream from inside the house? If I hit her, was she hurt?* I felt sick, like I was going to throw up the hot dog and the soda. I hung my head down and tried to breathe deeply and slowly.

I need to go back, I thought. *I can't leave someone hurt.* That would be going from vandalism to something totally different.

I began the walk back to the house. Every step was slow and it seemed to take forever. When I got there, I walked up to the door. The porch was sagging so bad that I thought it might cave in on me at any moment. I could see the broken window through the huge hole in the porch's roof. My shoes crunched on the broken glass from the window I'd busted.

This is so stupid! I thought. *I should go home.*

Okay, I'd try the door but if it was locked, I'd be out of there.

I turned the handle. It was rusty, but it opened. *Great.* I pushed the door forward and it scraped across the floor.

The stairs inside didn't look like they would hold me and I wondered again how I always seemed to end up in these messes. From upstairs, I heard a faint scraping noise and a sob. There was definitely someone here.

The stairs were crumbling in places, and I carefully made my way up them. It was a small house, empty except for a few pieces of rotted furniture and some boards here and there.

I walked into a bedroom with the broken window. There was a stool by the window and sitting on it was a woman. She was very old and hunched over, holding her shoulder.

I wanted to run. *What do I say to her? How can I possibly make up for this?*

I turned to leave, but she looked up and saw me. "Hello?" she said, more of a question than a statement.

"Uh, hi," I managed, as I considered how fast I

could get down the stairs.

"I'm hurt, my shoulder," she said. I could see tears in her eyes.

I took a breath and walked toward her. My words began to tumble out faster than I could hold them in. "I'm really sorry. I didn't
know anyone was here. The house looks so bad. They dared me to throw it. I'm really sorry."

I knelt beside her. She had the softest eyes and the kindest face I'd ever seen. Her hair was speckled with gray and she reached out with her good arm to touch me as if I were a ghost.

"It hurts. Did you throw that rock at me?" She was resting her hand on my shoulder and I was afraid. At the same time, I felt like she was my grandmother. Her face was so warm and I was drawn to her.

"I'm really sorry. I didn't know you were here."

"Why wouldn't I be here, honey? I'm always at the house. I never leave except for Sundays when we have church. You know that, Paulie," she laughed. "You feeling okay?"

Paulie? Who is that? I didn't understand. "My

name's Luke," I said.

She looked at me as if she suddenly didn't know me, and she removed her hand from my shoulder. After a moment of staring, she asked, "Who are you?"

"I'm one of the neighborhood boys. I live down the street. My name is Luke," I repeated.

"Not my Paulie," she said. "I swear I don't know why I forget everything nowadays."

"Are you hurt bad?"

She rubbed her hand across her arm where the rock grazed her. "It hurts a little but I'll be okay. I'm hungry more than anything. I guess I forgot to go grocery shopping and there's nothing to eat in the kitchen. The house seems really dirty, too."

Did she not realize the house was abandoned and no one had been there for years? It seemed crazy that she acted like it was her home. Maybe she was homeless and thought of the place as her own. Out of guilt, I asked her, "Would you like me to bring you some food?"

"Oh, Paulie!" Then she paused. "I mean, Luke. Yes, that would

be nice. I will wait here for you. I'm very tired

today."

"Yes, Ma'am. I'll be right back." I made my way down the crumbling stairs and out the front door. I planned to bring this lady some food and then I'd consider us even. But things don't always turn out the way we think they are going to, especially for me.

4

I was almost to my house when Lark and Terence appeared.

"Did you actually go inside that house?" Lark asked.

"So, you guys ran off and watched me from somewhere safe? Glad I have such great friends. Thanks a lot!" I pushed my way between them and headed for home.

They followed me. "Well, I didn't know when you broke the window it would be that loud," said Terence.

"Or that there was someone inside!" said Lark, her eyes wide.

"Who was it?"

"An old lady. I think she's homeless or something. She kept calling me Paulie."

Terence and Lark followed me into the house and sat down at the kitchen table while I made a sandwich.

"Paulie? Who's that?" Terence asked, staring at the sandwich.

"How would I know? I'm just the one who hit an old lady with the rock you dared me to throw."

"Technically, it was Lark who dared you. Who's that sandwich for?" Terence asked, changing the subject.

"The lady," I said, shrugging.

"You're going back there? You're crazy! She's probably called the police and everything by now," Terence said.

"Whatever. I broke the window. I hit the old lady, and then she said she was hungry. So, I'm going to give her a sandwich and then we're even, okay?"

They were starting to annoy me with all the questions, and I felt a little hurt that my friends had run off on me.

"Okay," said Lark. "Don't get all cranky. We'll go with you."

"Oh no we wont," said Terence. "You can, but I'm going home. I'm hungry." He stood up, made a peace sign with his hand, and disappeared out the door.

"You don't have to go with me," I said. In front of Lark, I didn't have to be cool like I did for Terence. She understood me. "I have to do this, police or not. I feel bad. I shouldn't have thrown that rock."

"Okay," was all she said, and she stood up and helped me finish the sandwich, then put it in a bag. We found a bottle of juice in the pantry and headed out to the abandoned house. Neither one of us spoke, wondering if Terence was right.

The place was probably surrounded with cop cars, lights flashing and sirens blaring. I would be sent to some school for boys or something and never see my friends again.

When we came around the corner to the house, it sat there alone. No police, no one even driving up and down the lonely street.

We went inside, then upstairs carefully. The lady was still there, sitting on the stool. She looked lonely and confused, but her face brightened when she saw us.

"My Paulie," she said. "What a good boy you are."

I decided it wasn't worth it to keep telling her I was not Paulie. Besides, if she tells someone what I did, it's best to be Paulie so my mom would never find out.

Lark stepped forward and handed her the sandwich. The lady looked surprised to see another person.

"Well, who are you? Did you bring a friend, Paulie?" she asked, taking the sandwich. "What a pretty young lady. What's your name?"

"Lark," she answered.

"Nice to meet you, Lark. I'm Miss Wanda Rose." She started on the sandwich. "I'm so hungry," she said between bites. "It feels like I haven't eaten in days."

"Do you live here?" I asked.

"Yes, honey. You know that." She continued to eat the sandwich and I sat down on the floor in front of her. Lark joined me. Miss Wanda Rose had a voice like a song, and it made us both want to hear her talk.

"How long have you lived here, Miss Wanda Rose?" Lark asked.

"I was born in this house, me and my sister, Ella Rose," she said. She stared at the wall for a moment, chewing. "Ella Rose died a very long time ago. Do you know where all my furniture is? This place is a mess and I think someone may have stolen my things," she said, dropping her voice as if the intruder may still be nearby.

"I don't think anyone has lived in this house for a very long time. It's in very bad shape and I think it's dangerous to stay here," I said. Maybe we were the ones who needed to call the police, but I was still afraid this lady was going to realize I was Luke, the vandal that broke her window and nearly took her arm off with a rock.

"Well, I'm not leaving, Paulie," she said, sticking her lip out like a child and folding her arms in front of her.

"I was just trying to say that the house seems like it may fall in on us," I said.

"It may be a little dirty, but I'm not leaving. I told you that already," she huffed. "Stop arguing with me now, Paulie."

It was pointless to fight with her and so we sat silently while she ate.

We stayed with Miss Wanda Rose until she finished the sandwich and the juice. Then we said goodbye and started home. We left her sitting on the stool, playing with the wrapping on the juice bottle.

"I think something is wrong with her," said Lark, when we were out the door. "She thinks you're Paulie and she is all alone in that disaster of a house. It's not right."

"Yeah, but I don't know what to do," I said. "You heard her.

She's not leaving."

"Well, you better do something about this," said Lark. "She's an old lady. She can't stay in a house like that long without getting really hurt. Old people fall down all the time. Maybe you were meant to help her."

I thought about what Lark said as I went inside my house. And that night at dinner when my mom asked me what I'd been up to that day. And when I lay in bed.

Was I meant to help Miss Wanda Rose? How was

I going to explain the rock, the window, and the bruise on her arm? And besides, what can a kid do anyway?

5

I worried about Miss Wanda Rose. *What if she fell down the stairs? What if she told the police about the boy who threw the rock?*

On Saturdays, my mom always made pancakes with fruit in them. Bananas, strawberries, blueberries; I never knew what it would be. We'd sit at the kitchen table and laugh and talk. It was my favorite time of the week because I had my mom's full attention and she seemed less stressed.

This Saturday, she knew something was wrong as soon as I sat down. My eyes were bloodshot from a night of worrying. At first, we didn't talk much. I poured the juice and set the table. She finished making the pancakes. Blueberry. They smelled so good, but I was not hungry.

My mind was turning and turning over and over, wondering whether or not I should tell Mom what happened. I didn't want to get into more trouble after our battle about the skateboard. At the same time, I couldn't stop thinking that Miss Wanda Rose might get hurt in that rotting house.

Mom sat down. "I want to talk to you about the skateboard," she started. "I'm going in early tomorrow to work some overtime, and I'll have the money to pay for your new skateboard this Friday."

"Mom," I said, but she interrupted me.

"Luke, I know how important the skateboard is to you, and I am sorry we got into an argument about it. Let's just put it behind us, okay?"

"Thank you," I said, staring at the table. When I

didn't get

excited about the prospect of a new skateboard, she realized there was more on my mind.

She reached out and put her hand on mine. "What's wrong? I thought you'd be thrilled. Is something else going on?"

Should I tell her? Now she'd given me even more reason to keep a secret from her. If I told her what I did, she would change her mind and there would never be a new skateboard.

"Nothing," I said, picking at a blueberry in the one pancake on my plate. On any other Saturday, I'd have eaten about half a dozen already.

"I know something's up. You're not eating. You love Saturday breakfasts."

"I'm just not that hungry today."

She reached up and felt my forehead for a fever. "Are you getting sick?"

I wouldn't meet her gaze. "No." The stakes were too high for me to say anything else.

My mother leaned back in the chair and looked

hard at me. I could feel her staring and thinking, even without meeting her gaze. For someone who never spent much time with me, my mom sure did know exactly how to extract information. She should have been an interrogator for the military or something.

"Okay, let's play it this way. The skateboard is not an issue. Whatever it is, I will not go back on my word to get you the new board on Friday. And as long as you haven't killed anyone, no restriction, either. There's something on your mind and you can't keep things inside or you'll go crazy."

Suddenly, I felt free to tell her and I was grateful to have someone to talk to. I was still a little nervous that she would go back on her word to buy me the board. She didn't usually change her mind like that, though.

"Okay," I took a breath. "Yesterday, Lark and Terence and I were at this old, abandoned house, and they dared me to throw a rock and break a window. There were a bunch of windows broken in the house already." I looked up at her for the first time to see if she was going to explode with anger, but she looked calm so far. "They dared me, Mom. And then I threw the rock and it went through the window. But there's more."

She leaned forward, interested.

I was starting to get really nervous and thought I'd made a mistake, but it was too late now. "When I threw the rock, it hit someone inside. I swear I didn't know anyone was in there!" My voice started to get higher as I got more defensive and afraid.

She didn't say a word, like a professional. It made me talk even faster. "It was a woman. An old woman," I said. Her eyes were starting to get wider now. "At first, I ran off, but then I went back and went inside. She was sitting on a stool and she kept calling me Paulie."

"What happened then?" she asked.

"Well, she wasn't really hurt, just more surprised by the rock. We talked a little, and then she said it was her house and that people had taken her stuff and that she was hungry. So, I came home and got her a sandwich and then took it to her. I think she's homeless or something."

I felt relieved we'd skipped the vandalism part of the story and gone to the old woman part.

"Where is she now?" my mother asked.

I began to think I had done something wrong again but I wasn't sure what. "She said she wasn't leaving that house for nothing, so I think she's still there."

"In an abandoned house? That's no place for an old woman. What do you plan to do about it?" asked my mom.

I was surprised that she was leaving the decisions up to me. *Aren't grown ups supposed to take over and handle things?*

"I guess I should go over there and see if she's still there.

Maybe we could call the police? I don't know."

"I think you are right, Luke. We'll go together. Finish your pancake, and I'll pack a breakfast for her. If she is there, we will help her."

"Am I in trouble?" I asked.

"No. I'm disappointed that you took such a stupid dare, but you may learn a good lesson from this. Maybe this is meant to be." She packed a breakfast, and we headed out the door to see Miss Wanda Rose.

6

On the way to the house, I told Mom more about Miss Wanda Rose and about the house. Mom thought it was too dangerous for her to stay in a house that was falling apart, and we should work together to get her to come out. We arrived at the house and went inside. Mom carefully made it up the rotting steps.

We found Miss Wanda Rose sitting on the stool and looking out the broken window. She seemed not to hear us as we came into the room.

"Hi, Miss Wanda Rose," I said. She turned to look at us. She watched us for what seemed like an hour, and there was confusion in her eyes. Slowly, the confusion faded. "I've seen you before," she said.

"I was here yesterday," I said, giving her the pancakes. "I'm
Luke."

"Oh, yes," she said. "You brought that pretty girl with you." Then she looked at my mom. "She sure has gotten older!"

We all laughed. My mother helped her put syrup on the pancakes and introduced herself. "We thought maybe you'd like to take a walk after breakfast," she said. "It's a beautiful day."

"That sounds nice," she said as she ate. "I sure am hungry. Somebody took all my stuff and there is no food here. I don't know what happened. It's a mess here."

"Do you have family nearby?" my mother asked her.

"I have a daughter named..." her voice trailed off, and I could see she was thinking hard about it. "Virginia!" She seemed pleased to remember. "Yes, she is my daughter and she lives on Carter Street. I haven't seen her in a while. Maybe she is out of town. She usually comes by to visit. My Paulie used to come by, too, but he died a few years ago. He was such a good boy. You remind me of him," she said, pointing at me.

"Yes, you called me Paulie yesterday," I said, looking at the floor.

"I forget a lot of things. My daughter said I have Old Timer's disease." She changed the subject. "I just love pancakes. You are very sweet to bring them to me."

We sat with Miss Wanda Rose as she ate. Between bites, she told us about her childhood growing up in the house. The house was her home all her life, but she couldn't figure out why it was in such bad shape and all her things were missing.

Mom and I wondered what happened to her. It just didn't make sense for her to be there alone with no one to help her.

My own grandmother died with the disease, and she did not know me at all at the end. I was only six at the time, so I don't remember much. We would visit her in the nursing home, and she wouldn't know who I was. My mother always left there crying, and one day she said we would not be going back to the home because my grandmother had died. I never knew my grandfather or my grandparents on my dad's side of the family.

"Your dress looks like it needs washing," said my mother. "It's very dirty."

"Yes, I suppose it is," Miss Wanda Rose said. "I was waiting for Paulie to come and take me to church. I always put on a clean dress when he comes over. Do you know my Paulie? Are you friends of his?" she asked.

I could tell that she was forgetting who we were again.

Yesterday, she'd gotten stubborn and refused to leave.

I never thought before what it must be like to lose your memory. Strange people talking to you and telling you they are your friends and your relatives. That must be really tough. No wonder she got angry and didn't want people telling her what to do.

I felt sorry for her, and I wanted to help her. If she had family, they must be looking for her. I leaned over to my mother. "If she has a daughter on Carter Street, I could go look for her," I offered.

"Luke, that's a great idea. First, let's see if we can get her out of this house. It is dangerous to be in a house like this, especially for someone her age."

"Miss Wanda Rose, it's time to go for your walk now." In one quick motion, my mother was at her side, helping her up before she could protest. "We need to get some fresh air and sunshine, and I am going to get you a clean dress today," she added.

Miss Wanda Rose looked confused, but she did not fight my mother. "Well, okay," she said. "But we have to be back before Paulie gets here. I don't want to miss him. He's such a good boy, you know."

"Yes, I do know," said my mother, nodding her head. "Luke here is going to help you get down the stairs and outside. Well be back before Paulie gets here."

I helped Miss Wanda Rose down the steps, my heart pounding. I don't think I've ever prayed more in my life than I did with each slow step down those stairs. Each step groaned and creaked as if it were about to give way. There were 13 steps to the bottom, and I will never forget them.

We made it to the front door of the house and my mother opened it and led the way out onto the walk. Miss Wanda Rose paused to look back at the house. "My, it sure is in need of some repairs. Paulie, be a good boy and help me fix up the house when we get back."

I'd become Paulie again, but this time, I really didn't mind. She loved him, that was clear. I felt proud to be helping her.

My mother whispered to me that we were going to walk her to our house and then I could go search on Carter Street for her daughter, Virginia. If I could not find anyone on that street, we would call the police to come and help us.

Slowly, we moved along our street and to our house. Miss Wanda Rose did not walk fast. Sometimes she would stop walking and turn around to look back for her house.

"We sure are walking a long way. You know, my Virginia lives somewhere near here," she said. "Have you met my Virginia? She is such a good girl."

My mother was great at getting Miss Wanda Rose to keep moving forward and talking. I realized for the first time how kind and gentle she was. I knew she was nice, but I never saw her as anything more than my mom. Now, I saw how kind she was to Miss Wanda Rose, and how good she was at caring for her and keeping her moving.

I was a little afraid of Miss Wanda Rose. Afraid that she would decide she wasn't going to walk any further and afraid that she would go back to the house. It was weird to me that an adult would act like a child, and it made me uncomfortable.

My mother took it easily and guided her right down the street. I was impressed by it all.

We reached our house and led her inside. "My, what a pretty house you have," she said. "I sure am tired from that long walk. Are we going back now?"

"Not right away," my mother said. "Why don't we sit and rest for a moment before we walk back. Would you like a cup of tea?" "Why that sounds lovely," she said to my mother, and she made herself comfortable on the couch.

Mom instructed me to go to Carter Street and see if there was a Virginia living there who was missing her mother.

I was nervous about knocking on doors and asking people about Miss Wanda Rose, but I knew it was the right thing to do.

I headed out the door. On the way to Carter Street, I thought about what Lark had said. *Maybe you were meant to help her.*

7

Carter Street was only a few streets over from my house. Most of the houses in our neighborhood looked the same. Small, two-story brick buildings built in the 1950s when the factory was here. The factory closed in the 1980s and many people were out of work. Most of the people who lived here couldn't afford to sell their houses, so they just stayed and tried to make it while working two or more jobs. Us kids got left behind when the parents had to work.

Some of the houses were abandoned, some

were well maintained. But most were just normal, aging homes. There were about twenty houses on Carter Street. I decided to go down one side and up the other, house to house.

I made my way to the first house on Carter Street and knocked on the door. No one answered. I tried the second house. I heard a big dog barking inside and someone scrambling and yelling for the dog to get away from the door. A man in a bathrobe with a cigar in his mouth peeked his head out of the cracked door. He was obviously annoyed.

"What do you want, kid? You selling something?" he barked.

I gulped. I hadn't really thought about what I was going to say if someone answered the door and here was this huge guy staring down at me.

"Uh, no..." I started.

"Well, spit it out then," he said, trying to keep the huge dog from charging through the door and eating me whole.

"I'm looking for someone named Virginia," I said. "Her mother is Miss Wanda Rose."

"Never heard of her, kid." He disappeared behind the door, the dog still barking and scratching the floor with his claws.

Okay, two down and about 18 to go, I thought. Door number three was also no answer. No answer at door number four.

At the fifth house, a young woman holding a baby answered. "What can I do for you?" she asked.

"I'm looking for a woman named Virginia. Her mother is Miss
Wanda Rose."

"Oh, I know Virginia," she said. "We both have vegetable gardens and we share the harvest with each other. Her mother has been missing for several days now. They are afraid she is dead. She has Alzheimers and she wandered off. What a shame," she said, shaking her head.

My heart skipped a beat. *There was a Virginia! And she was looking for her mother.* I was so excited to find her and tell her that I'd found Miss Wanda Rose. "Where does she live?" I asked, bouncing up and down on my toes.

"Across the street. The one with the yellow door. It's the only one with a yellow door on our street. Virginia painted the door yellow so that she would know which house was theirs. Sometimes she forgot which house was the right one."

I followed her pointing finger and saw the house with the bright yellow door. I bolted off the steps in one big leap.

In the middle of the street, I turned to the lady in the doorway. "Thanks!" I waved to her and ran for the yellow door.

I rang the bell. Nothing. I waited. I rang the bell again. Then I heard footsteps and a voice said, "I'm coming." I shifted from one foot to the other, eager to meet Virginia.

She opened the door. She was a small, older woman with graying hair and a smile I recognized as the same one on Miss Wanda Roses face.

"Uh, Miss Virginia? I asked, suddenly very nervous.

"Yes," she said.

I didn't know how to say it, so I just blurted out, "I found Miss
Wanda Rose."

Her eyes grew wide with surprise and then worry. She was missing for several days and Virginia feared the worst. She stood there, looking at me, unable to speak.

"She was at an abandoned house on my street, and I found her there." Then I quickly added, "She's okay. She's at my house right now."

I wasn't expecting the response that Miss Virginia gave me. She practically fell on me, hugging me. I could hear her sniffles as she began to cry.

"I've been so worried," she said between sobs. "We looked everywhere, but the police stopped searching for her yesterday. They said there was nothing they could do. I thought she was gone forever."

It was uncomfortable for this woman to be holding me and crying, especially since everyone in the street could see. I glanced behind me and saw that the woman with the baby across the street was watching us, her hand to her mouth.

"Would you like to go see her?" I asked, hoping she would stop holding me and crying on my shirt.

"Oh, yes. Thank you, son," she said. She went

inside and got her purse. When she reappeared, she was wiping her face with a handkerchief. She locked her door and took my arm to help her down the stairs.

When we were on the street, she asked me a question. "How did you find my mother in the house? The police said they went by a few days ago and no one was there."

My stomach knotted. I was not looking forward to telling someone else the story. It wasn't even lunchtime and already it had been a very long day. "Well, "I started. "My friends and I were sitting in front of the house and they dared me to throw a rock and break a window. We thought the house was abandoned. I didn't know she was in there. I'm really sorry. The rock broke the window and hit her in the arm."

Her grip on my arm tightened, and I was surprised at her strength.

I could see the surprise in her face, so I quickly added, "She isn't hurt or anything. The rock just grazed her." Relief came across Miss Virginia's face, and her grip on my arm relaxed a little. I finished telling her how I went inside and how my mother went over today and convinced her to come home with us.

"My mother was a stubborn woman before the

Alzheimers, let me tell you. She never did anything she didn't want to do. Some days are really bad. She behaves like a child and refuses to do anything she's asked to do."

I smiled, remembering how Miss Wanda Rose stuck out her lip like a toddler and refused to leave the house the day before. "Yes Ma'am. We tried to get her to leave yesterday, but she refused."

"I had no idea she was in that house. It's falling apart and needs to be torn down. My mother can't go wandering back there or she could get really hurt. She's been gone four days now. I just can't believe you found her."

I nodded to her and helped her cross the street to my house. We went inside and found Miss Wanda Rose, leaning on the pillows of the couch and sleeping soundly.

Miss Virginia started to weep again, covering her mouth to quiet the sobs. She didn't want to wake her mother. Mom introduced herself and she and Miss Virginia went to the kitchen for tea. I followed along, suddenly hungry for those blueberry pancakes.

A Skateboarding Story

8

The next day, I sat outside with Terence and Lark. Terence was practicing a new skateboard trick called an Ollie Impossible. To do the trick, he put one foot on the back of the board and the other in the middle. He pushed down with his back foot like he was doing an Ollie to pop the board in the air, but instead, he spun the board in a circle around his back foot and landed back where he started. Terence almost had it, but his feet kept landing one on the board and one off. He was really close to sticking it.

"So, what happened with the old lady?" Lark asked.

"Her name is Miss Wanda Rose," I said defensively.

"Sorry," she said, rolling her eyes at me. "So, what happened to

Miss Wanda Rose?"

"We brought her home. You should have seen my mom. She was able to get her to walk all the way to our house without one complaint. It was awesome," I said with pride.

Lark stopped. "Wow, that's cool."

Terrence joined in. "My grandpa had the Old Timers. They start acting like kids and they get real mad if you make them do stuff they don't want to. Its rough."

"My grandma had it, too, but I never saw her much. I never realized how hard it must be to live with all that," I said.

The conversation was getting too heavy for Lark, so she changed the subject. "When do you get your new skateboard? Is it a good one?"

"Mom said I could pick it out myself. I'd like an Alien Workshop board. Their graphics are sick."

"Yeah," said Terence. "But I don't know how long

they last. I heard they chip easy."

"You could go with a Flip," Lark said. "I hear their boards have great pop."

"I'm not really into their graphics. Element has some good ceramic bearings but they are expensive. I don't think my mom is going to go that high. I may end up with a Complete."

"It's better to build a skateboard yourself from scratch than to buy a Complete," Terence said.

"Yeah, if you're rich," I said. "Maybe someday I'll own my own skate shop and I can do anything I want."

On Friday, I got my new skateboard. An Alien Workshop with a Rob Dyrdek logo on it. We spent the weekend doing tricks any place we could find.

On Sunday evening, I came home to find Miss Virginia and Miss Wanda Rose in our living room. Mom invited them for dinner. I was glad to see them both.

"Hello, Paulie," said Miss Wanda Rose as she hugged me. "You're such a good boy."

I laughed and hugged her back. It wasn't so bad to be Paulie.

Virginia seemed relieved that I didn't mind going along with Miss Wanda Rose. She'd lost her son and wanted me to be Paulie, and that was okay with me. I missed having a grandma anyway.

They talked about the weather and about the lack of jobs in our town.

"There's never anything for kids to do around here," I chimed in.

Miss Wanda Rose asked, "What types of things do you do for fun?"

I wasn't sure if she was talking to me or to Paulie, and I had no idea what things Paulie had done as a child. "My favorite thing to do is skateboard," I told her. "My mom just bought me a new skateboard. I broke my other one."

"I'd love to see it," said Miss Virginia.

"Really?" I was used to being run off by adults. This was great! I showed her the skateboard. It was blue with 3 sets of white aliens on it, and it had Rob Dyrdek's name under the aliens. It was an expensive board and I was very proud of it.

"Are those aliens?" Miss Wanda Rose asked. "That's crazy!" She laughed, rubbing her hand over the bottom of the board. "It is a very nice skateboard. Show me your stuff. Come over to my house and ride out front, and I will sit on the steps and watch you."

I had trouble closing my wide-open mouth and finding something to say. An adult actually interested and asking to see me skateboard? "Wow. Yes, Ma'am. I'd like that a lot. My friends will come, too."

"You do that. I get so bored in the house all day. The fresh air will do me good."

Dinner went well and I was excited to tell Lark and Terence about how cool Miss Wanda Rose was, even though she had a bad memory. They were as surprised as me to learn that someone was interested in seeing us skateboard.

A couple of days later, on a warm Friday afternoon, we all walked over to Miss Virginia's house. I helped Miss Wanda Rose on to the steps and she sat down.

"Show me some moves!" she said, waving her arms around in circles. We all laughed.

That was all we needed to begin showing off every trick we knew. It was the most fun we'd had all summer, doing tricks and laughing with Miss Wanda

Rose. Some of the neighbors came out and sat on the steps to watch us as well.

Terence told me later that he felt like a superstar that day. Finally someone was paying attention to us.

I skated past and did a Heel Flip, flipping my board in a sideways loop. I landed it perfectly and kept on going. Terence rode past, doing an Ollie, and then coming back and doing a Half Cab with a little bit of a pop. His board sailed around in a 180-degree turn as he jumped in the air.

Lark was next. She skated past, doing a North Ollie with the board coming up in front of her, and then she came back by with a South Ollie, with her foot going off the back of the board.

Miss Virginia came out with fresh squeezed lemonade and some cookies. One of the neighbors suggested that we start coming by every Friday afternoon to show off our new tricks. For the rest of the summer, we made our Friday afternoon appointment to skateboard in front of Miss Virginia's house to entertain Miss Wanda Rose.

The summer ended and we went back to school. The days got colder and shorter, and we stopped going to Miss Virginia's house to skateboard. Miss Wanda Rose got very sick with the flu and her memory got even worse. She was still a happy, warm woman, but most of the time she looked at people and had no idea who they were. She was also having trouble getting around and doing things for herself.

One Saturday, Miss Virginia came by the house to talk to Mom and me. "My mother is getting sicker and having fewer days when she knows who anyone is. But one thing she does talk about often is you, Luke. She says that you were meant to be in her life. This summer you spent entertaining her and giving her a purpose has been so good for her. I want to give you a gift, and I know Miss Wanda Rose would want you to have it as well."

I gulped. *A gift? What could she possibly want to give me?*

"The house you found my mother in belongs to us. It hasn't been lived in for many years because she moved in with me after Paulie died. The house needs to be torn down because it is dangerous. I've discussed it with mother in the times when she seems to understand, and we've agreed that we want to tear the house down and build a small skate park there for the neighborhood kids."

No way. It couldn't be real. I didn't know what to

say. "Wow," was all that came out.

"Now, it will take some work from you, Luke," she said, taking my hand. "We don't have a lot of money, so you'll need to find people with skills to help us tear down the house and clean the lot. And you'll need to make some kind of plan for whatever you need to make it into a skate park."

My mind started thinking about all the fun we could have with our own place to skate. But I also knew it would be a lot of work.

"I'm ready to work hard," I said. And I leaned over and hugged her tightly and whispered, "Thank you." Tears were in my eyes.

I'd never gotten such an awesome present in my life.

9

That winter, Terence, Lark, and I planned out the new skate park. We asked friends and neighbors to help us tear down the house and get supplies to build a place for us to skate. Once we started asking people for help, we found lots of people who were willing to pitch in. Many knew someone who could do the hardest parts, like tearing down the house and laying a concrete foundation.

Mom took us to a skate park in the city, and they offered to help us plan the layout of our skate park. A hardware store donated pipes for us to use for grinding on. Terence had an uncle who drove a concrete truck. He said we could have any leftover concrete he had in his truck at the end of the day.

It all came together the next summer. We managed to salvage some of the parts of the house to build a platform and the frames for a set of stairs. Terence's uncle brought concrete day after day. We worked hard every night to smooth and set the fresh concrete. Mom brought some men from work to help us clean up the debris from the demolished house.

The neighborhood Boy Scout troop held a fundraiser to get the supplies to make two park benches for us. It was incredible to see our community come together and help us build a place for the neighborhood kids to play.

Miss Wanda Rose came a few times to watch us build the park. She did not remember at this point that her house had been on the lot where we were working. She didn't talk much any more and she stopped calling me Paulie. She smiled at me warmly, but she didn't know me anymore. Miss Virginia said she was in the last stages of Alzheimers and soon she would not be able to go outside any more.

It was difficult for her to walk and she spent a lot of time sleeping.

We decided to make August fourth the day we would officially open the park. It was Miss Wanda Rose's birthday. We taped off the park with a big spool of red ribbon. My mother made a cake and many of the neighbors came with snacks and drinks.

The day before, Terence, Lark, and I made a special surprise of our own. On one side of the park, there was a small ramp. Our surprise was hidden under an old blanket, waiting for Miss Wanda Rose to arrive.

That afternoon, after the hottest part of the day disappeared, we all met at the park. Terence was there with his mother. Lark and her dad were there. After we set up, we saw Miss Virginia arrive in her car with Miss Wanda Rose. We helped her put the wheelchair together and get Miss Wanda Rose into it comfortably. She smiled at us, but we could tell she was confused and tired.

"Happy ninetieth birthday," we all said to her.

She smiled and looked around at all of us. We sang a birthday song and she clapped her hands at the end. "So nice," she said. "So nice."

She had taken to repeating those words over and over lately. Sometimes she had an entire conversation with someone just with those two words.

We wheeled Miss Wanda Rose over to the skateboard ramp and everyone joined us.

"Miss Wanda Rose," I said. "We love you and we wanted to thank you for giving us this cool place to hang out." Terence and Lark positioned themselves on either side of the blanket. "You will always be remembered here." I motioned for them to lift the blanket.

There was a gasp from everyone and Miss Wanda Rose leaned forward in her wheelchair. "So, so nice. So nice. Nice!" She clapped her hands again.

On the ramp was Miss Wanda Rose's name, written in graffiti style, and a cartoon picture of her smiling at everyone. We'd gotten some of the kids in the art club at school to help us paint it the day before. It was awesome, with huge, rounded letters making up her name in blue and yellow. Everyone started clapping and I could see Miss Virginia wiping her eyes and smiling.

We helped Miss Wanda Rose hold a pair of scissors and cut the ribbon, officially opening the park. Everyone clapped again and then moved out of the way for the skateboarders to fill the park. I helped Miss Virginia wheel Miss Wanda Rose back to the car. She was slumping over a little in her seat, obviously tired from the excitement.

"She would be so proud of you," said Miss Virginia.

"I know. It's okay."

"So nice," whispered Miss Wanda Rose, her eyes closed.

Mom and I helped her get into the car and Mom went home with them to help out.

I sat down on one of the benches. "It *is* so nice," I said. I couldn't believe about a year ago I was throwing a rock into a window. Today I was sitting in the same place at a really awesome skate park.

Lark came over and sat down beside me. "See, you *were* meant to help her, and she was meant to help you."

I laughed and nodded.

"And you can thank me because I was the one who dared you. You could paint my picture on the other ramp when we get it built," she said, smiling. "I dare you."

About The Author

Tammy Griffith is a new writer whose first book, Miss Wanda Rose: A Skateboarding Story, was entered into the 2014 Story Shares contest. The book won Best Character Based Story, and inspired her to work on writing more books for teens and young adults. "My youngest son is a struggling reader, and he worked with me to write the book," says Tammy. "It was an amazing experience for us both."

About The Publisher

Story Shares is a nonprofit focused on supporting the millions of teens and adults who struggle with reading by creating a new shelf in the library specifically for them. The ever-growing collection features content that is compelling and culturally relevant for teens and adults, yet still readable at a range of lower reading levels.

Story Shares generates content by engaging deeply with writers, bringing together a community to create this new kind of book. With more intriguing and approachable stories to choose from, the teens and adults who have fallen behind are improving their skills and beginning to discover the joy of reading. For more information, visit storyshares.org.

Easy to Read. Hard to Put Down.

A Skateboarding Story

www.ingramcontent.com/pod-product-compliance
Lightning Source LLC
Chambersburg PA
CBHW060144050426
42448CB00010B/2298